Shadow Dance

Shadow Dance

Poems of the night for young people

Collected by Adrian Rumble

Illustrated by Rowena Allen

Cassell

Cassell Educational Limited
Artillery House, Artillery Row
London SW1P 1RT

821.9

SAINT BENEDICT SCHOOL
DUFFIELD ROAD
DERBY DE22 1JD

(10757

**Since this page cannot accommodate all the copyright
notices pages 110–12 constitute an extension of the
copyright page.**

This selection © 1987 Adrian Rumble
Illustrations © 1987 Cassell Educational Limited
First published 1987

British Library Cataloguing in Publication Data

Shadow dance: poems.
   1. Children's poetry, English
   I. Rumble, Adrian
   821'.914'0809282   PR1195.C47

ISBN 0–304–31493–5

Printed in Great Britain by Biddles Limited, Guildford

This one is for my lovely lady,
with love and gratitude.
'May you build a ladder to the stars
And climb on every rung
And may you stay forever young.'
Bob Dylan

Contents

8

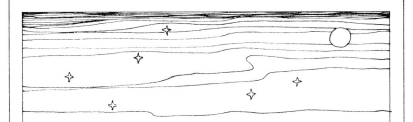

Come with me now

Adrian Rumble

Come with me now
as daylight ends;
the sun sinks low,
black night descends;
into a world of sleep and dream,
moon and starshine
and lamplight gleam.
Enter now and join the dance
of creeping shadow
and midnight trance.
This is the dark kingdom
where colours change,
streets grow longer
and mystery reigns.
Enter now and join the dance.

Shadow Dance

Ivy O Eastwick

O Shadow,
Dear Shadow,
Come, Shadow,
And dance!
On the wall
In the firelight
Let both of
Us prance!
I raise my
Arms, thus!
And you raise
Your arms, so!
And dancing
And leaping
And laughing
We go!
From the wall
To the ceiling,
From ceiling
To wall,
Just you and
I, Shadow,
And none else
At all.

Torches

John Cotton

It is the torches I remember best.
Going home on a winter's evening
We would point them skyward,
Screwing the fronts
To sharpen the pencils of light
That they might pierce the darkness the better.
Bold young challengers of stars
We competed in length and brightness.
Yes, better than the chips
Tart with vinegar and salt grains,
In bags like small grease-proof hats,
Better even than the large orange bottles,
'Tizer' tasting of fruit that never was,
Were the torches,
Their beams like friendly knives
Making cuts in a darkness
Which oh so quickly healed
At the touch of a switch.

Night Shapes

Paddy Kinsale

Outside is full of cats and darkness,
Howling screeches and thick black stillness,
Things creeping silently,
Bats shuddering restlessly,
Owls hooting,
Moles rooting.

Outside is full of black shapes moving,
Shadows weird and slowly passing,
Things watching the dark,
Eyes looking for work,
Figures stealing,
Night brooding.

Outside is full of people dreaming,
Hoping, muttering, turning and scheming,
Ideas moving in the mind,
Voices uttering no sound,
Time slipping,
Dawn looming.

Posting Letters

Gregory Harrison

There are no lamps in our village,
And when the owl-and-bat black night
Creeps up low fields
And sidles along the manor walls
I walk quickly.

It is winter;
The letters patter from my hand
Into the tin box in the cottage wall;
The gate taps behind me,
And the road in the silver of moonlight
Gleams greasily
Where the tractors have stood.

I have to go under the spread fingers of the trees,
Under the dark windows of the old man's house,
Where the panes in peeling frames
Flash like spectacles
As I tip-toe.
But there is no sound of him in his one room
In the Queen-Anne shell,
Behind the shutters.

I run past the gates,
Their iron feet gaitered with grass,
Into the church porch,
Standing, hand on the cold door ring,

While above
The tongue-tip of the clock
Clops
Against the hard palate of the tower.
The door groans as I push
And
Dare myself to dash
Along the flagstones to the great brass bird,
To put one shrinking hand
Upon the gritty lid
Of Black Tom's tomb.

Don't tempt whatever spirits stir
In this damp corner,
But
Race down the aisle,
Blunder past font,
Fumble the door,
Leap steps,
Clang iron gate,
And patter through the short-cut muddy lane.

Oh, what a pumping of breath
And choking throat
For three letters.
And now there are the cattle
Stirring in the straw
So close.

I can hear their soft muzzling and coughs;
And there are the bungalows,
And the steel-blue miming of the little screen;
And the familiar rattle of the latch,

And our own knocker
Clicking like an old friend;
And
I am home.

from November Night

Adelaide Crapsey

Listen . . .
With faint dry sound,
Like steps of passing ghosts,
The leaves, frost-crisped, break from the trees
And fall.

17

Hurry Home

Leonard Clark

You had better hurry home for your supper's nearly
    ready,
Your mother's in the kitchen and she's awfully wild,
She's been shouting at the cat, and she keeps on
    saying,
'O where has he got to, the wretched child?'

She has been to the front door and looked through the
    window
And now she's banging on the frying pan,
The plates and the dishes are all on the table,
So run, my boy, as fast as you can.

Don't you know she's cooking your favourite supper,
Potatoes in their jackets and beefsteak pie?
She's made a jug of custard for the pudding in the
    oven,
Get a move on, Joe, the stars are in the sky.

They've all left the factory, the streets will soon be
    empty,
No more playing now, it's time you fed,
It really is a shame to keep your mother waiting,
So come have your supper, and then off to bed.

Windy Nights

Robert Louis Stevenson

Whenever the moon and stars are set,
   Whenever the wind is high,
All night long in the dark and wet,
   A man goes riding by.
Late in the night when the fires are out,
Why does he gallop and gallop about?

Whenever the trees are crying aloud,
   And ships are tossed at sea,
By, on the highway, low and loud,
   By at the gallop goes he.
By at the gallop he goes, and then
By he comes back at the gallop again.

Fish and chips

L T Baynton

Heading for the light, bitter cold night,
Round this corner – smell it now?
Windows steamed like fog inside.
Hungry queue all bags in hands.
Old papers piled but not to read,
Giant sized salt and vinegar near,
And wooden forks like babies' toys.
Nearer now, oh hear the hiss,
And on the shelf the golden plaice, the chips.
At last my turn, my mouth is wet –
No thanks, not wrapped – hot in my hand.
Outside the night seems warmer now,
Until – I hold a crumpled paper ball.
Why do they go so soon?

Flashlight

Judith Thurman

My flashlight tugs me
through the dark
like a hound
with a yellow eye,

sniffs
at the edges
of steep places,

paws
at moles'
and rabbits'
holes,

points its nose
where sharp things
lie asleep –

and then it bounds
ahead of me
on home ground.

Stopping by Woods on a Snowy Evening

Robert Frost

Whose woods these are I think I know.
His house is in the village though;
He will not see me stopping here
To watch his woods fill up with snow.

My little horse must think it queer
To stop without a farmhouse near
Between the woods and frozen lake
The darkest evening of the year.

He gives his harness bells a shake
To ask if there is some mistake.
The only other sound's the sweep
Of easy wind and downy flake.

The woods are lovely, dark and deep,
But I have promises to keep,
And miles to go before I sleep,
And miles to go before I sleep.

The Sounds in the Evening

Eleanor Farjeon

The sounds in the evening
Go all through the house,
The click of the clock
And the pick of the mouse,
The footsteps of people
Upon the top floor,
The skirts of my mother
That brush by the door,
The crick in the boards,
And the creak of the chairs,
The fluttering murmurs
Outside on the stairs,
The ring of the bell,
The arrival of guests,
The laugh of my father
At one of his jests,
The clashing of dishes
As dinner goes in,
The babble of voices
That distance makes thin,
The mewings of cats
That seem just by my ear,
The hooting of owls
That can never seem near,
The queer little noises
That no one explains . . .
Till the moon through the slats
Of my window-blind rains,

And the world of my eyes
And my ears melts like steam
As I find in my pillow
The world of my dream.

Street at Night

Thomas Young

Not a sound came from the street
Just some silently stepping feet
Going farther and farther
Growing fainter and fainter
Till they had gone in the distance
　　and could be heard no more.

The Park

James S Tippett

I'm glad that I
    Live near a park
For in the winter
    After dark
The park lights shine
    As bright and still
As dandelions
    On a hill.

Rainy Nights

Irene Thompson

I like the town on rainy nights
    When everything is wet –
When all the town has magic lights
    And streets of shining jet!

When all the rain about the town
    Is like a looking-glass,
And all the lights are upside-down
    Below me as I pass.

In all the pools are velvet skies,
    And down the dazzling street
A fairy city gleams and lies
    In beauty at my feet.

November Night

Corinna Rumble

Smells of hot potatoes
cooking in the cool night air;
rockets, roman candles shoot
up into the dark sky.
A frightened rabbit scurries home
fighting the ferocious wind
while shouts of laughter
echo through the air.
The heat of the bonfire
warms everyone
but soon dies down.
The people go home.
Jack Frost pays a visit
through the night,
covers up the ground
with a blanket of frost.
He moves swiftly
across the fields
and covers fallen leaves.
A hen clucks and screeches
as a fox approaches slyly
behind her back.
She tries to escape . . . too late!
The fox grabs and eats the hen.
All that remains
is a mass of feathers.
The fox leaves the chicken-run
and scampers off into the night.

Bedtime

Charlotte Zolotow

The day is over
the night comes gently
the bathtub water
is green and warm

the little girl comes down the stairs
gaily
shining from her bath
like a Christmas ball

the fire dances for her
like a princess swaying swaying

and her mother when she kisses her goodnight
is soft
with pillow smell

she hears the wind ruffling outside
saying sleep sleep sleep.

Awake and Dreaming

Joanna Rumble

I wake from a nightmare.
I feel restless
but the nightmare
still clings to me.
I toss and turn
trying to shake it off.
Suddenly I jump up
and out of bed.
I'm wide awake now.
I open the window;
a moonbeam peers through.
Through the window I see
the silhouette of the almond tree,
a fox silently slipping by;
its scarlet coat shimmers
in the light of the moon.
I hear a rustle –
a cat is rummaging
through the dustbin.
I begin to feel drowsy,
I drag myself into bed.
I begin to dream,
but NO!
it's not a nightmare,
it's a dream
of all the wonderful things
I have seen tonight.

My Dream

Anon

I dreamed a dream next Tuesday week,
   Beneath the apple-trees;
I thought my eyes were big pork-pies,
   And my nose was Stilton cheese.
The clock struck twenty minutes to six,
   When a frog sat on my knee;
I asked him to lend me eighteenpence
   But he borrowed tenpence of me.

Old Man of Peru

Anon

There was an old man of Peru
Who dreamed he was eating his shoe.
   He woke in the night
   in a terrible fright,
And found it was perfectly true.

Mars

Anon

And then in my dream I slipped away
To the silver ship in the dawn of day,
To the grasshopper men with their queer green
    eyes
And suits that glittered in splendid dyes.
They came, they said, from a thirsty land,
A land that was dead and choked with sand;
The wells were empty and dusty and dry,
And the burning sun hung low in the sky;
'We are old,' they said. 'We have had our day,
And the silent cities crumble away.'
'Yet here,' they said, 'we may find again
All that was carefree and lovely then
When the wells were full and the cities rang
With the harvest song that the reapers sang!'

          · · ·

Oh, when I'm a man I shall travel to Mars
In a silver ship, in a night of stars,
And there I shall see those grasshopper men.
Without any doubt I shall know them again.

I dreamt I caught a little owl

Christina Rossetti

'I dreamt I caught a little owl
And the bird was blue –'

'But you may hunt forever
And not find such a one.'

'I dreamt I set a sunflower
And red as blood it grew –'

'But such a sunflower never
Bloomed beneath the sun.'

Counting Sheep

Wes Magee

They said,
'If you can't get to sleep
   try counting sheep.'
I tried.
It didn't work.

They said,
'Still awake! Count rabbits, dogs,
   or leaping frogs!'
I tried.
It didn't work.

They said,
'It's *very* late! Count rats,
   or red-eyed bats!'
I tried.
It didn't work.

They said,
'Stop counting stupid sheep!
   EYES CLOSED! DON'T PEEP!'
I tried
and fell asleep.

Whistle, daughter, whistle

Anon

Whistle, daughter, whistle,
And you shall have a sheep.
Mother I cannot whistle,
Neither can I sleep.

Whistle, daughter, whistle,
And you shall have a cow.
Mother I cannot whistle,
Neither know I how.

Whistle, daughter, whistle,
And you shall have a man.
Mother I cannot whistle
But I'll do the best I can.

The Attack

Leonard Clark

When I have settled down in bed
And pulled the sheets over my head,

I know that I am safe inside
And from Red Indians can hide,

Who by their hawk-eyed chief are sent
To gallop round and round my tent

Bareback upon their stallions,
Whooping loud and firing guns

All across the rolling plain
Out of sight and back again.

But when I come up for some air
There are redskins everywhere,

On the warpath, near my head,
Circling round and round the bed,

And then I hide myself until
They have gone and all is still.

Things that go 'bump' in the night

Spike Milligan

Things that go 'bump' in the night,
Should not really give one a fright.
It's the hole in each ear
That lets in the fear,
That, and the absence of light!

How Far?

Olive Dove

'How far away
Is the evening star?'
'Ask the night horse.
He knows how far.

Talk to him gently.
Give him honey and hay
And seven bells for his bridle
And he will take you away.

Snorting white fire
He will stream through the air
Past mountains of the moon
And the rainbow's stair.

And if you go singing
Through the dark and the cold
Your purse will be filled
With silver and gold.'

Dreamland

Walter de la Mare

Annie has run to the milldam,
Annie is down by the weir;
Who is it calling her name, then?
Nobody else to hear?
Cold the water, calm and deep,
Honey-sweet goldilocks half-asleep,
Where the green-grey willows weep,
Annie is down by the weir.

Rain

Walter de la Mare

I woke in the swimming dark
And heard, now sweet, now shrill,
The voice of the rain-water,
　　Cold and still,

Endlessly sing; now faint,
In the distance borne away;
Now in the air float near,
　　But nowhere stay;

Singing I know not what,
Echoing on and on;
Following me in sleep,
　　Till night was gone.

The Battle

Shel Silverstein

Would you like to hear
Of the terrible night
When I bravely fought the –
No?
All right.

A Spell for Sleeping

Alastair Reid

Sweet william, silverweed, sally-my-handsome.
Dimity darkens the pittering water.
On gloomed lawns wanders a king's daughter.

Curtains are clouding the casement windows.
A moon-glade smurrs the lake with light.
Doves cover the tower with quiet.

Three owls whit-whit in the withies.
Seven fish in a deep pool shimmer.
The princess moves to the spiral stair.

Slowly the sickle moon mounts up.
Frogs hump under moss and mushroom.
The princess climbs to her high hushed room,

Step by step to her shadowed tower.
Water laps the white lake shore.
A ghost opens the princess's door.

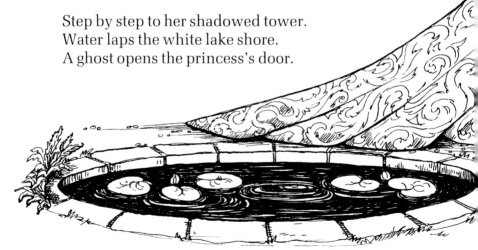

Seven fish in the sway of the water.
Six candles for a king's daughter.
Five sighs for a drooping head.
Four ghosts to gentle her bed.
Three owls in the dusk falling.
Two tales to be telling.
One spell for sleeping.

Tamarisk, trefoil, tormentil.
Sleep rolls down from the clouded hill.
A princess dreams of a silver pool.

The moonlight spreads, the soft ferns flitter.
Stilled in a shimmering drift of water,
Seven fish dream of a lost king's daughter.

Buses

Michael Rosen

Late last night
I lay in bed,
driving buses
in my head.

Dreams

J Charles

What did you dream of last night?
Dolls and toys and joys so bright,
and blossoming trees.

What are you dreaming tonight?
Of love and marriage and delight,
and leafy trees.

What will you dream of tomorrow?
Wrinkles and loneliness and sorrow,
and leafless trees.

What did I dream?

Robert Graves

What did I dream? I do not know –
    The fragments fly like chaff.
Yet strange, my mind was tickled so
    I cannot help but laugh.

Pull the curtains close again,
    Tuck me grandly in;
Must a world of humour wane
    Because birds begin

Complaining in a fretful tone,
    Rousing me from sleep –
The finest entertainment known,
    And given rag-cheap?

Owls

Leonard Clark

They stare at you,
these ugly phantoms of the night,
and do not seem to care
if you stare back at them.
All day they perch, half asleep,
in lonely ruins, dark church towers,
not liking the sun,
dozing, and dreaming with stupid face,
of scurrying mice, fat beetles, baby birds,
swallowed greedily in one cruel gulp.

At twilight they come out.
Like floating paper glide along lanes,
noiselessly dipping over hedges,
or fanning their ghostly way
around the houses, down the avenues,
ears and eyes set for the kill.
Then, gorged with fresh meat,
they sag back home,
the moon's eye watching them,
hooting in the wind,
waiting for the next raw victim.

I do not like owls.
I shiver when I hear them
screeching at the bottom of the garden,
invading the darkness,
glad I'm not a mouse,
small bird or beetle.

from At Night in the Wood

Nancy M Hayes

The Stoat, the Rat
And the squeaking Bat
All open their keen little eyes
And rise.
And the Hedgehog peeps from his cosy nest
And hurries out with the rest.
The bark of the Fox shows he's astir,
And the Rabbit shivers within his fur.

The Bat

Theodore Roethke

By day the bat is cousin to the mouse.
He likes the attic of an ageing house.

His fingers make a hat about his head.
His pulse is so slow we think him dead.

He loops in crazy figures half the night
Among the trees that face the corner light.

But when he brushes up against a screen,
We are afraid of what our eyes have seen:

For something is amiss or out of place
When mice with wings can wear a human face.

The Bird of Night

Randall Jarrell

A shadow is floating through the moonlight.
Its wings don't make a sound.
Its claws are long, its beak is bright.
Its eyes try all the corners of the night.

It calls and calls: all the air swells and heaves
And washes up and down like water.
The ear that listens to the owl believes
in death. The bat beneath the eaves,

The mice beside the stone are still as death.
The owl's air washes them like water.
The owl goes back and forth inside the night,
And the night holds its breath.

Night Walk

Max Fatchen

What are you doing away up there
On your great long legs in the lonely air?
   Come down here, where the scents are sweet,
   Swirling around your great, wide feet.

How can you know of the urgent grass
And the whiff of the wind that will whisper and
     pass
   Or the lure of the dark of the garden hedge
   Or the trail of a cat on the road's black edge?

What are you doing away up there
On your great long legs in the lonely air?
   You miss so much at your great, great height
   When the ground is full of the smells of night.

Hurry then, quickly, and slacken my lead
For the mysteries speak and the messages speed
   With the talking stick and the stone's slow
     mirth
   The four feet find on the secret earth.

51

Prowler

Vera Wyse

At night my black cat
Walks on roofs and walls.
Her silent figure
Creeps and crawls,
Pounces and devours
Hapless mice
And abandoned baby birds.

At dawn the waking sun
Creeps over roofs and walls.
Lying in the garden
Are last night's corpses,
Mute witness to the
Shadowy hunter that
Kills by night.

Batty Friends

Vera Wyse

At dusk the bats,
Flittery flutterers
Squeaking and stuttering
Twirling and turning
And skirling and whirling,
Catch all the gnats
That dance round our heads,
That whine and stab
And bite.
The itchery witchery
Blood sucking
Pests.

The Cat

W H Davies

Within that porch, across the way,
   I see two naked eyes this night;
Two eyes that neither shut nor blink,
   Searching my face with a green light.

But cats to me are strange, so strange –
   I cannot sleep if one is near;
And though I'm sure I see those eyes
   I'm not so sure a body's there.

The Tom-cat

Don Marquis

At midnight in the alley
A Tom-cat comes to wail,
And he chants the hate of a million years
As he swings his snaky tail.

Malevolent, bony, brindled,
Tiger and devil and bard,
His eyes are coals from the middle of Hell
And his heart is black and hard.

He twists and crouches and capers
And bares his curved sharp claws,
And he sings to the stars of the jungle nights,
Ere cities were, or laws.

Beasts from a world primeval,
He and his leaping clan,
When the blotched red moon leers over the roofs,
Give voice to their scorn of man.

He will lie on a rug tomorrow
And lick his silky fur,
And veil the brute in his yellow eyes
And play he's tame, and purr.

But at midnight in the alley
He will crouch again and wail,
And beat the time for his demon's song
With the swing of his demon's tail.

'Whistle and I'll come to thee'

Adrian Rumble

A breathless night,
still and cold,
a full moon shone,
cruel and old.
I found a whistle
by the sea:
'Whistle and I'll come to thee.'

I laughed and blew
with all my might . . .
a gale sprang up
and ripped the night,
whipped the water
into waves,
smashed ships on rocks
and into caves;
racing madly
down the shore
it shouted inland
with a roar;
trees and houses,
church and town,
the whole world
was crashing down.

At last the dawn
brought peace . . .
I stood and stared:
my house was gone,
the land lay bare.
I hurled the whistle
far away,
for all I know
it still lies there.
'Whistle and I'll come to thee.'

WHISTLE IF YOU DARE!

Midnight Wood

Raymond Wilson

Dark in the wood the shadows stir:
   What do you see? –
Mist and moonlight, star and cloud,
Hunchback shapes that creep and crowd
   From tree to tree.

Dark in the wood a thin wind calls:
   What do you hear? –
Frond and fern and clutching grass
Snigger at you as you pass,
   Whispering fear.

Dark in the wood a river flows:
   What does it hide? –
Otter, water-rat, old tin can,
Bones of fish and bones of a man
   Drift in its tide.

Dark in the wood the owlets shriek:
   What do they cry? –
Choose between the wood and river;
Who comes here is lost forever,
   And must die!

The Hairy Toe

Traditional American

Once there was a woman went out to pick beans,
and she found a Hairy Toe.
She took the Hairy Toe home with her,
and that night, when she went to bed,
the wind began to moan and groan.
Away off in the distance
she seemed to hear a voice crying,
'Where's my Hair-r-ry To-o-oe?
Who's got my Hair-r-ry To-o-oe?'

The woman scrooched down,
'way down under the covers,
and about that time
the wind appeared to hit the house,

smoosh,

and the old house creaked and cracked
like something was trying to get in.
The voice had come nearer,
almost at the door now,
and it said,
'Where's my Hair-r-ry To-o-oe?
Who's got my Hair-r-ry To-o-oe?'

The woman scrooched further down
under the covers
and pulled them tight around her head.

The wind growled around the house
like some big animal
and r-r-um-mbled
over the chimbley.
All at once she heard the door cr-r-a-ack
and Something slipped in
and began to creep over the floor.

The floor went
cre-e-eak, cre-e-eak
at every step that thing took towards her bed.
The woman could almost feel
it bending over her bed.
Then in an awful voice it said:
'Where's my Hair-r-ry To-o-oe?
Who's got my Hair-r-ry To-o-oe?
You've got it!'

The Witch

Mary Coleridge

I have walked a great while over the snow,
And I am not tall nor strong.
My clothes are wet, and my teeth are set,
And the way was hard and long.
I have wandered over the fruitful earth,
But I never came here before.
Oh, lift me over the threshold, and let me in at the
    door!

The cutting wind is a cruel foe.
I dare not stand in the blast.
My hands are stone, and my voice a groan,
And the worst of death is past.
I am but a little maiden still,
My little white feet are sore.
Oh, lift me over the threshold, and let me in at the
    door!

Her voice was the voice that women have,
Who plead for their heart's desire.
She came – she came – and the quivering flame
Sank and died in the fire.
It never was lit again on my hearth
Since I hurried across the floor,
To lift her over the threshold, and let her in at the
    door.

Queen Nefertiti

Anon

Spin a coin, spin a coin,
　All fall down;
Queen Nefertiti
　Stalks through the town.

Over the pavements
　Her feet go clack,
Her legs are as tall
　As a chimney stack;

Her fingers flicker
　Like snakes in the air,
The walls split open
　At her green-eyed stare;

Her voice is thin
　As the ghosts of bees;
She will crumble your bones,
　She will make your blood freeze.

Spin a coin, spin a coin,
　All fall down;
Queen Nefertiti
　Stalks through the town.

Halloween

Marie Lawson

'Granny, I saw a witch go by,
I saw two, I saw three!
I heard their skirts go swish, swish, swish –'

　　'Child, 'twas leaves against the sky,
　　And the autumn wind in the tree.'
'Granny, broomsticks they bestrode,
Their hats were black as tar,
And buckles twinkled on their shoes –'

　　'You saw but shadows on the road,
　　The sparkle of a star.'

'Granny?'
　　'Well?'
'Don't you believe – ?'
　　'What?'
'What I've seen?
Don't you know it's Halloween?'

The House on the Hill

Wes Magee

It was built years ago
By someone quite manic
And sends those who go there
Away in blind panic.
They tell tales of horrors
That can injure or kill
Designed by the madman
Who lived on the hill.

> If you visit the House on the Hill for a dare
> Remember my words . . . 'There are dangers.
>   Beware!'

The piano's white teeth
When you plonk out a note
Will bite off your fingers
Then reach for your throat.
The living room curtains
– long, heavy, and black –
Will wrap you in cobwebs
If you're slow to step back.

> When you enter the House on the Hill for a dare
> Remember my words . . . 'There are dangers.
>   Beware!'

The 'fridge in the kitchen
Has a self-closing door.
If it knocks you inside
Then you're ice cubes . . . for sure.
The steps to the cellar
Are littered with bones
And up from its darkness
Drift creakings and groans.

    If you go to the House on the Hill for a dare
    Remember my words . . . 'There are dangers.
      Beware!'

Turn on the hot tap
And the bathroom will flood
Not with gallons of water
But litres of blood.
The rocking chair's arms
Can squeeze you to death;
A waste of time shouting
As you run . . . out . . . of . . . breath . . .

    Don't say you weren't warned or told to take care
    When you entered the House on the Hill for a dare.

A Close Encounter

Adrian Rumble

I was returning from a friend's one night
when our street was bathed in a ghostly light
and an eerie drone filled the air.

My trembling hand clutched the gate, and there –
in the middle of the road – large and round
was a shining object touching down.

It shimmered and glowed as if alive;
made a humming and buzzing as if a hive
of bees was swarming inside.

Well, I tell you this and I swear it's no lie;
a trapdoor opened, a ladder swung down
and a strange looking creature wobbled down to
    the ground.

Its huge nodding head was a great bulbous dome.
It had one staring eye in a forehead of chrome
and it was looking straight at me.

Then it lifted up its lobster claw
and beckoned me gently to its door
slowly shifting its grasshopper legs.

It had no mouth but it made a noise
which must have come from a hidden voice.
Its electric crackle plainly said:

'We have come from Mars, the planet red.
We offer peace and friendship to every man.
You are welcome to visit our land, if you can.

Step inside, earthling. Do not be afraid.
We have ideas to exchange and thoughts to trade.
There is much to be learnt from each other.'

Though I knew the words he spoke were true,
I was much too frightened to know what to do.
So I fled up the path to our house.

A welcoming light, and my mum making toast.
'What on earth can be wrong?' said my dad.
'Have you just seen a ghost?'

Hallowe'en

Leonard Clark

This is the night when witches fly
On their whizzing broomsticks through the wintry
   sky;
Steering up the pathway where the stars are strewn,
They stretch skinny fingers to the waking moon.

This is the night when old wives tell
Strange and creepy stories, tales of charm and spell;
Peering at the pictures flaming in the fire
They wait for whispers from a ghostly choir.

This is the night when angels go
In and out the houses, winging o'er the snow;
Clearing out the demons from the countryside
They make it new and ready for Christmastide.

At the Keyhole

Walter de la Mare

'Grill me some bones,' said the Cobbler,
   'Some bones, my pretty Sue;
I'm tired of my lonesome with heels and soles,
Springsides and uppers too;
A mouse in the wainscot is nibbling;
A wind in the keyhole drones;
And a sheet webbed over my candle, Susie –
   Grill me some bones!'

'Grill me some bones,' said the Cobbler,
   'I sat at my tic-tac-to;
And a footstep came to my door and stopped,
And a hand groped to and fro;
And I peered up over my boot and last;
And my feet went cold as stones: –
I saw an eye at the keyhole, Susie! –
   Grill me some bones!'

Night Starvation *or* The Biter Bit

Carey Blyton

At night my Uncle Rufus
(Or so I've heard it said)
Would put his teeth into a glass
Of water by his bed.

At three o'clock one morning
he woke up with a cough,
And as he reached out for his teeth –
They bit his hand right off.

The will o' the wisp

Jack Prelutsky

You are lost in the desolate forest
where the stars give a pitiful light,
but the faraway glow of the will o' the wisp
offers hope in the menacing night.

It is lonely and cold in the forest
and you shiver with fear in the damp,
as you follow the way of the will o' the wisp
and the dance of its flickering lamp.

But know as you trudge through the forest
toward that glistering torch in the gloom
that the eerie allure of the will o' the wisp
summons you down to your doom.

It will lead you astray in the forest
over ways never travelled before.
If ever you follow the will o' the wisp
you'll never be seen anymore.

The Vampire

Jack Prelutsky

The night is still and sombre,
and in the murky gloom,
arisen from his slumber,
the vampire leaves his tomb.

His eyes are pools of fire,
his skin is icy white,
and blood his one desire
this woebegotten night.

Then through the silent city
he makes his silent way,
prepared to take no pity
upon his hapless prey.

An open window beckons,
he grins a hungry grin,
and pausing not one second
he swiftly climbs within.

And there, beneath her covers,
his victim lies in sleep.
With fangs agleam, he hovers
and with those fangs, bites deep.

The vampire drinks till sated,
he fills his every pore,
and then, his thirst abated,
licks clean the dripping gore.

With powers now replenished,
his thirst no longer burns.
His quest this night is finished,
so to his tomb he turns,

and there awhile in silence
he'll rest beneath the mud
until, with thoughts of violence,
he wakes and utters . . . blood!

The Bogeyman

Jack Prelutsky

In the desolate depths of a perilous place
the bogeyman lurks, with a snarl on his face.
Never dare, never dare to approach his dark lair
for he's waiting . . . just waiting . . . to get you.

He skulks in the shadows, relentless and wild
in his search for a tender, delectable child.
With his steely sharp claws and his slavering
   jaws
oh he's waiting . . . just waiting . . . to get you.

Many have entered his dreary domain
But not even one has been heard from again.
They no doubt made a feast for the butchering
   beast
and he's waiting . . . just waiting . . . to get you.

In that sulphurous, sunless and sinister place
he'll crumple your bones in his bogey embrace.
Never never go near if you hold this life dear,
for oh! . . . what he'll do . . . when he gets you!

The Troll

Jack Prelutsky

Be wary of the loathsome troll
that slyly lies in wait
to drag you to his dingy hole
and put you on his plate.

His blood is black and boiling hot,
he gurgles ghastly groans.
He'll cook you in his dinner pot,
your skin, your flesh, your bones.

He'll catch your arms and clutch your legs
and grind you to a pulp,
then swallow you like scrambled eggs –
gobble! gobble! gulp!

So watch your steps when next you go
upon a pleasant stroll,
or you might end in the pit below
as supper for the troll.

Green Man, Blue Man

Charles Causley

As I was walking through Guildhall Square
I smiled to see a green man there,
But when I saw him coming near
My heart was filled with nameless fear.

As I was walking through Madford Lane
A blue man stood there in the rain.
I asked him in by my front-door,
For I'd seen a blue man before.

As I was walking through Landlake Wood
A grey man in the forest stood,
But when he turned and said, 'Good day'
I shook my head and ran away.

As I was walking by Church Stile
A purple man spoke there a while.
I spoke to him because, you see,
A purple man once lived by me.

But when the night falls dark and fell
How, O how, am I to tell,
Grey man, green man, purple, blue,
Which is which is which of you?

At Night

Elizabeth Jennings

I'm frightened at night
When they put out the light
And the new moon is white.

It isn't so much
That I'm scared stiff to touch
The shadows, and clutch

My blankets: it's – oh –
Things long, long ago
That frighten me so.

If I don't move at all,
The moon will not fall,
There'll be no need to call.

But, strangely, next day
The moon slips away,
The shadows just play.

Haunted

William Mayne

Black hill
black hall
all still
owl's grey cry
edges shrill
castle night.

Woken eye
round in fright;
what lurks walks
in castle rustle?

Hand cold
held hand
the moving roving
urging thing;
dreamed margin

voiceless
noiseless
HEARD
feared
a ghost passed

black hill
black hall
all still
owl's grey cry
edges shrill
castle night.

The Mewlips

J R R Tolkien

The shadows where the Mewlips dwell
    Are dark and wet as ink,
And slow and softly rings their bell,
    As in the slime you sink.

You sink into the slime, who dare
    To knock upon their door,
While down the grinning gargoyles stare
    And noisome waters pour.

Beside the rotting river-strand
    The drooping willows weep,
And gloomily the gorcrows stand
    Croaking in their sleep.

Over the Merlock Mountains a long and weary way,
In a mouldy valley where the trees are grey,
By a dark pool's borders without wind or tide,
Moonless and sunless, the Mewlips hide.

The cellars where the Mewlips sit
    Are deep and dank and cold
With single sickly candle lit;
    And there they count their gold.

Their walls are wet, their ceilings drip;
    Their feet upon the floor
Go softly with a squish-flap-flip,
    As they sidle to the door.

They peep out slyly; through a crack
    Their feeling fingers creep,
And when they've finished, in a sack
    Your bones they take to keep.

Beyond the Merlock Mountains, a long and lonely
        road,
Through the spider-shadows and the marsh of Tode,
And through the wood of hanging trees and the
        gallows-weed,
You go to find the Mewlips – and the Mewlips feed.

Oft in the Lone Churchyard

Robert Blair

Oft in the lone churchyard at night I've seen,
By glimpse of moon-shine chequering through
    the trees,
The school-boy with his satchel in his hand,
Whistling aloud to bear his courage up,
And lightly tripping o'er the long flat stones,
(With nettles skirted, and with moss o'ergrown),
That tell in homely phrase who lie below.
Sudden he starts, and hears, or thinks he hears,
The sound of something purring at his heels;
Full fast he flies, and dares not look behind him,
Till out of breath he overtakes his fellows;
Who gather round, and wonder at the tale
Of horrid apparition, tall and ghastly,
That walks at dead of night, or takes his stand
O'er some new-opened grave; and (strange to
    tell!)
Vanishes at crowing of the cock.

The Way Through The Woods

Rudyard Kipling

They shut the road through the woods
Seventy years ago.
Weather and rain have undone it again,
And now you would never know
There was once a road through the woods
Before they planted the trees.
It is underneath the coppice and heath,
And the thin anemones.
Only the keeper sees
That, where the ring-dove broods,
And the badgers roll at ease,
There was once a road through the woods.

Yet, if you enter the woods
Of a summer evening late,
When the night-air cools on the trout-ringed
    pools
Where the otter whistles his mate,
(They fear not men in the woods,
Because they see so few.)
You will hear the beat of a horse's feet,
And the swish of a skirt in the dew,
Steadily cantering through
The misty solitudes,
As though they perfectly knew
The old lost road through the woods . . .
But there is no road through the woods.

Witch Goes Shopping

Lilian Moore

Witch rides off
Upon her broom
Finds a space
To park it.
Takes a shiny shopping cart
Into the supermarket.
Smacks her lips and reads
The list of things she needs:
  'Six bats' wings
  Worms in brine
  Ears of toads
  Eight or nine.
  Slugs and bugs
  Snake skins dried
  Buzzards' innards
  Pickled, fried.'
Witch takes herself
From shelf to shelf
Cackling all the while.
Up and down and up and down and
In and out each aisle.
Out come cans and cartons
Tumbling to the floor.
'This,' says Witch, now all a-twitch,
'Is a crazy store.
I CAN'T FIND A SINGLE THING
I am looking for!'

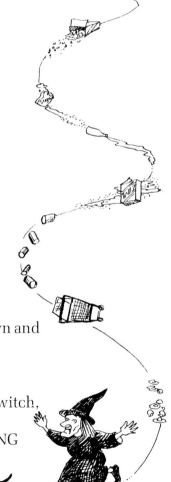

Fingummy

Mike Harding

Fingummy's fat
And Fingummy's small,
And Fingummy lives
With the boots in the hall.

If Fingummy bites,
If Fingummy tears,
If Fingummy chases you
Up the stairs

Shout 'Bumble-Bee Soup
And Bluebottle Jam.'
And run up to bed

                    can
              you
         as
     fast
as

Cos Fingummy lives
Where there's never no light
And Fingummy makes
The dark sounds of the night,
And Fingummy's fat
And Fingummy's small
And Fingummy lives
In the dark, in the hall.

The Grebs

Mike Harding

When at night in bed I sleep
I hear the Grebs around me creep.
I hear their whiskers scrape the floor,
I hear their fingers at the door.

I see their eyes shine in the dark,
I hear them squeal, I hear them bark.
'Oh Grebs, if you'll just go away,
I'll be good tomorrow, all day!'

But voices say 'Too late, too late!
We want you dead or alive!'
I tremble, shiver, shake and quiver
And beneath the bedclothes hide.

And feet and whiskers round me run
And closer, closer, closer come . . .
'Oh Grebs, if you'll just go away,
I'll be good tomorrow, all day!'
'Too late,
Too late,
We're here.'

The Haunted Lift

James Kirkup

On the ground floor
of this ultramodern
tower block

in the dead
middle
of the night

the lift doors
open, with a
clang.

Nobody enters,
and nobody
comes out.

In the dead
middle
of the night

the lift doors
close with a clang,
and the lift begins

to move
slowly
up . . .

with nobody in it,
nobody but
the ghost of a girl

who lived here once
on the thirteenth floor of
this ultramodern tower block.

One day, she went to play
in an old part of town,
and never came back.

She said she was just
going to the corner shop,
but she never came home.

Now her ghost
keeps pressing
in the dead

middle of the night
the button
for the thirteenth floor.

She gazes longingly
at the familiar landing,
but only for a moment . . .

then the lift doors
clang in her face
and her tears

silently flow
as the lift
in the dead

middle
of the night
so soft and slow

carries her down again
down below,
far, far below

the ground
floor, where nobody
waits for the haunted lift

in the dead
middle
of the night.

Sometimes
on the thirteenth floor
her mother and father

with her photo
beside their bed
wake up

in the dead
middle of the night, and hear
the mysterious clanging

of closing lift doors,
and wonder
who it could be

in the dead
middle
of the night

using the lift
at such
an unearthly hour.

In this ultramodern
tower block
there is no thirteenth floor.

Flying

J M Westrup

I saw the moon
One windy night,
Flying so fast –
All silvery white –
Over the sky,
Like a toy balloon
Loose from its string –
A runaway moon.
The frosty stars
Went racing past,
Chasing her on
Ever so fast.
Then everyone said,
'It's the clouds that fly,
And the stars and the moon
Stand still in the sky.'
But I don't mind –
I saw the moon
Sailing away
Like a toy
Balloon.

Stars at Night

Vera Wyse

Is there anybody there,
Up there up there,
Where the silent stars
Are frostily shining?
Is there anybody there?

Is there anybody there,
Up there up there?
I'm here at my window
Looking up there
Where the silent stars
Are frostily shining.
I'm ready to meet you.
Is there anybody there?

Is there anybody there,
Up there up there?
There's lots of us here
On the blue green planet
Wanting to meet you,
Needing your friendship,
Is there anybody there?

Is there anybody there,
Up there up there,
Where the silent stars
Are frostily shining?
Come and help us
On the blue green planet.
We need your wisdom,
We've none of it here.

Is there anybody there?
Is there anybody there?
Is there anybody?
Any body?
Any?
Body?

from Wind and Silver

Amy Lowell

Greatly shining,
The Autumn moon floats in the thin sky;
And the fish-ponds shake their backs and flash
   their dragon scales
As she passes over them.

Rags

Judith Thurman

The night wind
rips a cloud sheet
into rags,

then rubs, rubs
the October moon
until it shines
like a brass doorknob.

The Night Will Never Stay

Eleanor Farjeon

The night will never stay,
The night will still go by,
Though with a million stars
You pin it to the sky;
Though you bind it with the blowing wind
And buckle it with the moon,
The night will slip away
Like sorrow or a tune.

The Harvest Moon

Ted Hughes

The flame-red moon, the harvest moon,
Rolls along the hills, gently bouncing,
A vast balloon,
Till it takes off, and sinks upward
To lie in the bottom of the sky, like a gold doubloon.

The harvest moon has come,
Booming softly through heaven, like a bassoon.
And earth replies all night, like a deep drum.

So people can't sleep,
So they go out where elms and oak trees keep
A kneeling vigil, in a religious hush.
The harvest moon has come!

And all the moonlit cows and all the sheep
Stare up at her petrified, while she swells
Filling heaven, as if red hot, and sailing
Closer and closer like the end of the world

Till the gold fields of stiff wheat
Cry 'We are ripe, reap us!' and the rivers
Sweat from the melting hills.

February Twilight

Sara Teasdale

I stood beside a hill
  Smooth with new-laid snow,
A single star looked out
  From the cold evening glow.

There was no other creature
  That saw what I could see –
I stood and watched the evening star
  As long as it watched me.

The Falling Star

Sara Teasdale

I saw a star slide down the sky,
Blinding the north as it went by,
Too burning and too quick to hold,
Too lovely to be bought or sold,
Good only to make wishes on
And then forever to be gone.

The Horseman

Walter de la Mare

I heard a horseman
   Ride over the hill;
The moon shone clear,
The night was still;
His helm was silver,
   And pale was he;
And the horse he rode
   Was of ivory.

The Song of the Stars

from a Pasamaquoddy Indian song

We are the stars which sing.
We sing with our light.
We are the birds of fire.
We fly across the heaven.

Sing a Song of Science

Carey Blyton

Sing a song of science,
A rocket-full of mirth;
Four-and-twenty monkeys
Orbiting the earth.

When the rocket landed,
It came down on the moon,
And there they scoffed the Gruyère cheese
With knife and fork and spoon.

Surprise! or the escapologist

Carey Blyton

At the foot of the Apennine Mountains,
Where astronauts explore,
The curious Lunar Sea-squirt
Watches from its door.

And as they wander blithely
Around in their lunar cars,
The Sea-squirt steals their module –
And flies away to Mars.

Burning Burning Moonward

Adrian Rumble

Burning burning moonward
straight across the sky
deep into the universe
toward the moon on high.

Behind us now in blackness
Earth misty white and blue
lovely and abandoned
breathless bright and new.

Gliding gliding moonward
dancing through a void
turning to the music
of star and asteroid.

Gigantic looming satellite
pocked and cratered crust
silver ashen grey
cold rock and ancient dust.

Falling falling moonward
heart pounding in my chest
hiss of retro fire
and our spacecraft comes to rest.

'The Eagle has Landed'

Adrian Rumble

The airlock swings open –
behold! a new world:
obsidian black sky
lit by the sun's
fierce glare.
Inch
down the ladder –
the first man on the moon!
Look!
The first footprint.
Listen!
The first word
splitting the still dead silence.
Dead dust
dead rock
dead black sky.
A dead dead world.
Zombie in a moontrance I
trip
stumble
fall
rise
before the slow dust settles.
I leap in lingering arches.
Steady yourself.
Get your samples –
moondust moonrock.
Temperature check.

Humidity test.
And so
plod
carefully back.
My footprints in the ancient dust.

Venus

Adrian Rumble

Look up
towards the evening sky
just as the sun dies down;
see the planet Venus
sparkle like an emperor's crown.

Look out
across the morning sky,
just as the sun's reborn;
see the planet Venus
singing – in the dawn.

Escape at Bedtime

Robert Louis Stevenson

The lights from the parlour and kitchen shone out
    Through the blinds and the windows and bars;
And high overhead and all moving about,
    There were thousands of millions of stars.
There ne'er were such thousands of leaves on a
        tree,
    Nor of people in church or the park,
As the crowds of the stars that looked down upon
        me,
    And that glittered and winked in the dark.
The Dog, and the Plough, and the Hunter, and all,
    And the star of the sailor, and Mars.
These shone in the sky, and the pail by the wall
    Would be half full of water and stars.
They saw me at last, and they chased me with
        cries,
    And they soon had me packed into bed;
But the glory kept shining and bright in my eyes,
    And the stars going round in my head.

from The Moon was but a Chin of Gold

Emily Dickinson

The moon was but a Chin of Gold
A Night or two ago –
And now she turns Her perfect Face
Upon the World below –

Open Up Your Window

Adrian Rumble

Open up your window
and let the moon shine in;
the dust of night is dancing
to a bright white moonglow hymn.
Take the path of moonbeam,
step out, go on and climb;
all night's creatures wait for you
and they dance in starlit rhyme.
Oh join with us in dance of night
and listen, oh just listen
as the music binds you tight.
Enter worlds of wonder now;
join the midnight dance:
before too long the day will dawn
and end your sunless trance.
Embrace the kingdom of the moon
before it is too late.
The world of night will fade too soon;
don't wait, don't wait, don't wait.

Index of poets

Index of first lines

Acknowledgements

The editor and publisher wish to thank the following for permission to reprint copyright poems in this anthology. Although every effort has been made to contact the owners of the copyright in poems published here, a few have been impossible to trace. If they contact the publisher, correct acknowledgement will be made in future editions.

Robert Blair	Oft in the Lone Churchyard from *Hist Whist* published by Evans Bros. Reprinted by permission of the publisher.
Carey Blyton	Surprise! or the escapologist; Sing a Song of Science; Night Starvation *or* The Biter Bit. From *Bananas in Pyjamas* published by Faber & Faber Ltd. Reprinted by permission of the author.
Charles Causley	Green Man, Blue Man – from *The Collected Poems of Charles Causley* published by Macmillan London and Basingstoke. Reprinted by permission of David Higham Associates Ltd.
J Charles	Dreams from *Macmillan Poetry Pack I*. Reprinted by permission of Macmillan London and Basingstoke.
Leonard Clark	Halloween from *Good Company* by Leonard Clark. The Attack; Hurry Home; Here and There. From *Collected Poems and Verses for Children* by Leonard Clark. Both published by Dobson Books Ltd. Reprinted by permission of Dobson Books Ltd. Owls from *The Singing Time* by Leonard Clark published by Hodder & Stoughton Ltd. Reprinted by permission of Hodder & Stoughton Ltd.
John Cotton	Torches from *The Crystal Zoo* published by Oxford University Press. Reprinted by permission of the author.
W H Davies	The Cat from *The Complete Poems of W H Davies* published by Jonathan Cape Ltd. © the Executors of the W H Davies Estate. Reprinted by permission of the publisher and the Executors of the W H Davies Estate.
Walter de la Mare	Rain; Dreamland; At the Keyhole; The Horseman. Reprinted by permission of the Literary Trustees of Walter de la Mare and the Society of Authors as their representative.
Olive Dove	How Far? Reprinted by permission of the author.
Bob Dylan	Forever Young (extract). © 1973, 1974 by Ram's Horn Music. All rights reserved. International copyright secured. Reprinted by permission.
Max Fatchen	Night Walk from *Songs For My Dog and Other People* by Max Fatchen. (Kestrel Books 1980). © 1980 by Max Fatchen. Reproduced by permission of Penguin Books Ltd.

Eleanor Farjeon	The Sounds in the Evening; The Night Will Never Stay. From *Silver Sand and Snow* by Eleanor Farjeon published by Michael Joseph. Reprinted by permission of David Higham Associates Ltd.
Robert Frost	Stopping by Woods on a Snowy Evening from *The Poetry of Robert Frost*, ed. Edward Connery Lathem published by Jonathan Cape Ltd. © the Estate of Robert Frost. Reprinted by permission of the publisher and the Estate of Robert Frost.
Robert Graves	What did I dream? from *The Collected Poems of Robert Graves* 1975 published by Cassell & Co. Ltd. Reprinted by permission of A P Watt Ltd on behalf of the Executors of the Estate of Robert Graves.
Mike Harding	The Grebs; Fingummy. From *Up the Booaye Shooting Poocackies* by Mike Harding published by Robson Books Ltd. Reprinted by permission of Robson Books Ltd.
Gregory Harrison	Posting Letters from *Posting Letters* published by Oxford University Press. Reprinted by permission of the author.
Ted Hughes	The Harvest Moon from *Season Songs* by Ted Hughes published by Faber & Faber Ltd. Reprinted by permission of Faber & Faber Ltd.
Randall Jarrell	The Bird of Night from *The Bat-Poet* by Randall Jarrell (Kestrel Books 1977) © 1963, 1964 by Macmillan Publishing Co. Inc. Reproduced by permission of Penguin Books Ltd.
Elizabeth Jennings	At Night from *The Collected Poems of Elizabeth Jennings* published by Macmillan London and Basingstoke. Reprinted by permission of David Higham Associates Ltd.
James Kirkup	The Haunted Lift. Reprinted by permission of the author.
Amy Lowell	Wind and Silver (extract) from *The Complete Poetical Works of Amy Lowell* © 1955 Houghton Mifflin Co. © 1983 renewed by Houghton Mifflin Co., Brinton P Roberts Esq. and G D'Andelot Belin Esq. Reprinted by permission of Houghton Mifflin Co.
Wes Magee	Counting Sheep; The House on the Hill. Reprinted by permission of the author.
William Mayne	Haunted from *Ghosts* published by Hamish Hamilton Ltd. Reprinted by permission of David Higham Associates Ltd.
Spike Milligan	Things that go 'bump' in the night. Reprinted by permission of Spike Milligan Productions Ltd.